NATURE'S SERENITY

"Life may be an untold story
Life may be heroic poetry
Life may be a miraculous mystery
Life may be a heavy memory"

Contents

"A doctor beyond a doctor
Concentrates, over half a century
On one deadly symptom
A lethal virus, not uncommon -
Chemistry of Jealousy"

"A doctor beyond a doctor...
After half a century
In a lab, huge with formidable
Data without verge
What is the cure"

Contents

"Mistlike finest droplets drop
From nowhere, wrap me up
With mystique in dew drops
Zillions. None of them stops"

"We stroll on and on.
Me and Drizzle
Everything seems nothing
But a drizzle. Dazzling"

Selected LuCxeed Poems

Contents

"Hurricane Katrina rages,
blows in thirty feet high flood,
burying town by town
        but home's roof.
Catastrophe must be shocked
by a stark contrast"

Math & Music

"Our hero of Gallantry, of Chivalry,
dives into violent turbulence,
swallowed, disappears,
    reemerges, spared.
in the windstorm,
    wrestles with the tempest,
has pulled out ten lives
    from brink of death"

Contents

"The sunlight has dyed my hair
golden brown,
Shone upon my way all years round...
A poetic soul is ever young,
ever young.
Though soon the snow, the moon
Is to give me a silver crown."

"Night hushed whistling leaves
to be quiet
To listen to what a little girl
precisely said.
Clock stopped to note a moment...
...may have met the wisest
in her dream."

Contents

"Have you heard my cry,
 your bride
At the coming wedding? ...
Our life isn't so planned. No-."

"Coffin's almost failed to bear...
but wept...
'Dyllon hears you no more.
Though he must want to hug, to beg
You two: *Be strong. Live on*' "

Contents

"I'll see you no more,
though I've never
seen you before.
You left Life... 'How so?'
Pain lingers on shore.
Eyes sore."

Quote in art Calligraphy &
introduced poem title 40 - 41

"Do you believe
Couch is a magician,
at the center of Luxury,
chubby, solidly heavy,
to spare muscle's energy,
relieve intensity,
to feed the desire for Ego,
soothe anxiety?"

Contents

"Love holds the key to Paradise
where Spring conjures
infinite new life
Summer splashes around
without a raincoat
Autumn chuckles amidst
golden leaves
Sacredly true, as Love always is
(unless it is not Love)
everywhere Love goes
(unless one lets Love leave)"

"Little as I once was,
catching falling leaves,
climbing fallen trees,
I wondered where Nature was.
It seemed far, and far,
and beyond reach."

Contents

"How much Liberty do I have
to choose my parents
to choose my siblings
to choose my childhood...
Seemingly
(if not for all of us)
Fate rolls the dice"

Quote in art Calligraphy &
introduced poem title 44 - 45

"Fate bestows the child a fortune,
when Wealth is a curse
Knowledge pollutes...
Is it possible
when Fate rolls the dice
(if not for all of us)
we deliver our own move?"

Quote a poem to introduce the poem

Q
in art calligraphy

QUOTE "Its Own Contrary"
to introduce the poem

Life may be
an untold story
Life may be
heroic poetry
Life may be a
miraculous mystery
Life may be a
heavy memory

QUOTE "MATH & MUSIC"
to introduce the poem

Numbers
are sketched
into tones
Equations
stretched into tunes
I'm fond of faithful math
I hear my heart
humming
lyrical poems

QUOTE "CHEMISTRY OF JEALOUSY" to introduce the poem

A doctor
beyond a doctor...
After half a century
In a lab, huge
with formidable
Data without verge
What is the cure

QUOTE "CHEMISTRY OF JEALOUSY" to introduce the poem

A doctor
beyond a doctor
Concentrates
over half a century...
On one deadly symptom
A lethal virus,
not uncommon -
Chemistry of
Jealousy

QUOTE "ME AND DRIZZLE"
to introduce the poem

Mistlike finest
droplets drop
From nowhere
wrap me up
With mystique
in dew drops
Zillions. None
of them stops

QUOTE "ME AND DRIZZLE"
to introduce the poem

We stroll
on and on
Me and Drizzle
Everything seems
nothing
But a drizzle
Dazzling

Quote. "Catastrophe Shocked" to introduce the poem

– Hail to Hero

Hurricane Katrina rages,
blows in thirty feet high flood,
burying town by town
but home's roof.
Catastrophe must be shocked
by a stark contrast

Quote. "Catastrophe Shocked"
to introduce the poem

Our hero
of Gallantry, of Chivalry,
dives into violent turbulence,
swallowed, disappears,
reemerges, spared
in the windstorm, wrestles
with the tempest,
has pulled out ten lives
from brink of death
- Hail to Hero

QUOTE "SILVER CROWN"
to introduce the poem

The sunlight has dyed
my hair golden brown,
Shone upon my way
all years round...
A poetic soul is ever young,
ever young.
Though soon the snow, the moon
Is to give me a silver crown.

QUOTE "MET THE WISEST"
to introduce the poem

Night hushed whistling leaves to be quiet
To listen to what a little girl precisely said
Clock stopped to note a moment...
...may have met the wisest
in her dream

Quote "...Isn't So Planned"
to introduce the poem

Have you heard my cry,
your bride
At the coming wedding?
Our life isn't so planned.
No--.

Quote "...Isn't So Planned" to introduce the poem

Coffin's almost failed to bear
but wept ...
"Dyllon hears you no more.
Though he must want
to hug, to beg
You two: 'Be strong.
Live on...."

QUOTE "DON'T GO AWAY"
to introduce the poem

I'll see you no more,
though I've never
seen you before.
You left Life... "How so?"
Pain lingers on shore.
Eyes sore.

QUOTE "Couch Magician"
to introduce the poem

Do you believe
Couch is
a magician,
at the center of Luxury,
chubby, solidly heavy,
to spare muscle's energy,
relieve intensity,
to feed the desire
for Ego,
soothe anxiety?

QUOTE "Nature's Touch"

to introduce the poem

Little as I once was,
catching falling leaves,
climbing fallen trees,
I wondered
where Nature was.
It seemed far, and far,
and beyond reach.

QUOTE "Unless..."
to introduce the poem

Love holds the key to Paradise
where Spring conjures infinite new life
Summer splashes around without a raincoat
Autumn chuckles amidst golden leaves

Sacredly true, as Love always is
(unless it is not Love)
everywhere Love goes
(unless one lets Love leave)

Quote: "Fate Rolls the Dice i"
to introduce the poem

How much Liberty
do I have
to choose my parents
to choose my siblings
to choose my childhood...
Seemingly
(if not for all of us)
Fate rolls the dice

QUOTE "FATE ROLLS THE DICE ii"
to introduce the poem

Fate bestows
the child a fortune,
when Wealth is a curse
Knowledge pollutes...
Is it possible
when Fate rolls the dice
(if not for all of us)
we deliver our own move?

POEM

@Poetry in gallery®

poem in art

LuCxeed Poem

Math & Music

Math and Music

I'm fond of math
A fountain of logic's truths
I'm fond of music
A realm of rhapsodic hums

Melodies, enchanting
Summon single string
after string
Sketch numbers into tones
Stretch equations into tunes

LuCxeed Poem

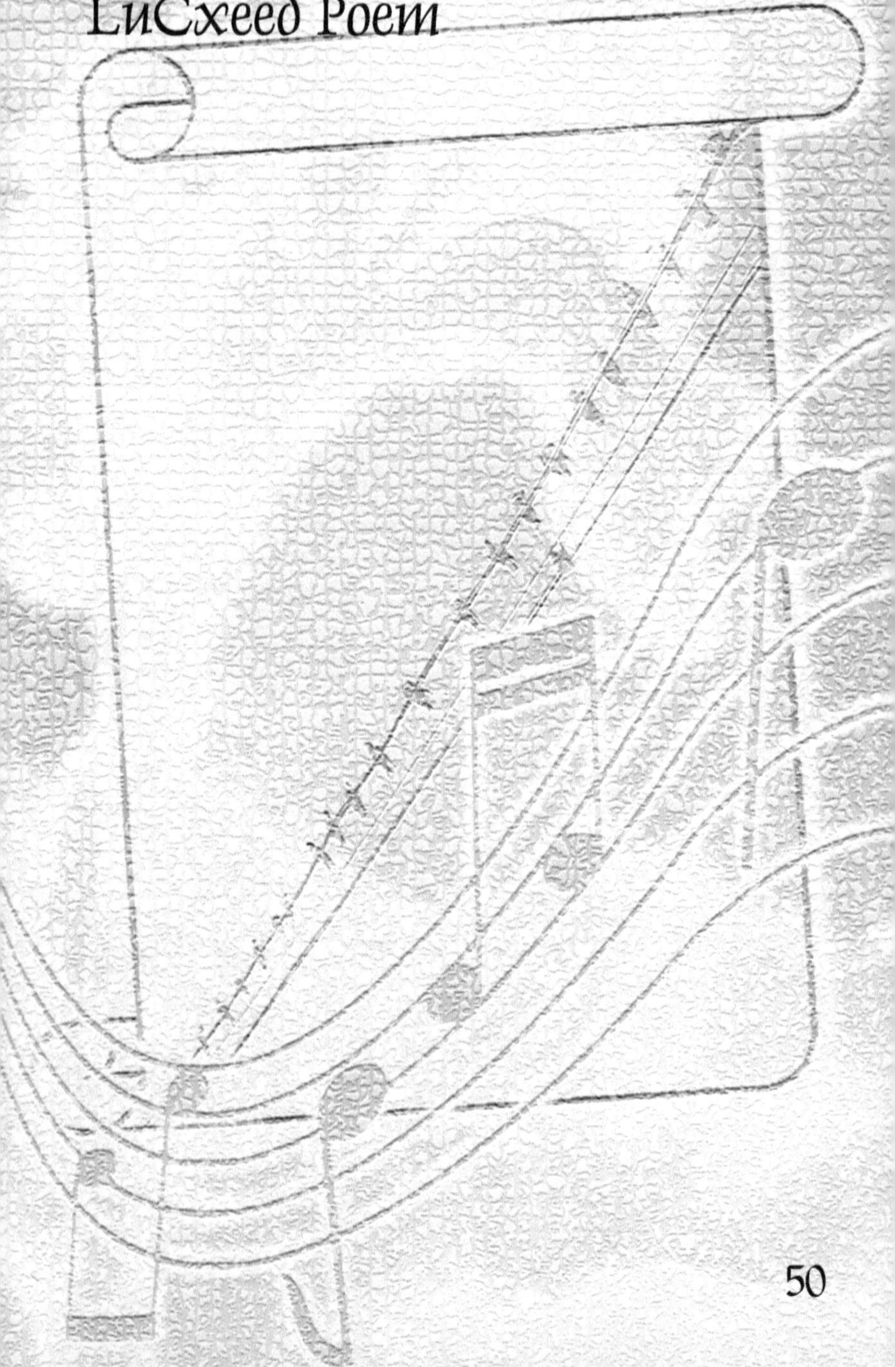

Math and Music

Spin chords of music
Compose the music of math
Math into poems,
simple truths
Into intricacy,
chaos into faith

Numbers are sketched
into tones
Equations stretched into tunes
I'm fond of faithful math
I hear my heart
humming lyrical poems

LuCxeed Poem

Its Own Contrary

Life may be
an untold story
Life may be
heroic poetry
Life may be
a miraculous mystery
Life may be
a heavy memory

Life at first has its cry
and at the last breath
Life meets its adversary
between, possibly often

Life is its own contrary

LuCxeed Poem

Hold your hand

Hold your Hand

My wish is so simple,
Just to hold your hand,
Yet, it is impossible.

We talk and walk
on the same earth,
Day and night.
We read and rest
on the same earth,
Day and night.

My dream is so humble,
Just to hold your hand,
Unbelievable, it is impossible.

LuCxeed Poem

Hold your Hand

We breathe the same air,
We bathe in
the same sunshine,
We wear the same blue sky,
We stroll under
the same moonlight.

Just want to hold your hand,
So simple, so humble,
Not forbidden,
yet impossible.

Linked Poem

chemistry of jealousy

Chemistry of Jealousy

A doctor beyond a doctor
Concentrates,
    over half a century
In a lab, formidably huge
Files piled upon files
    without verge
On one deadly symptom
A lethal virus,
    not uncommon -
Chemistry of Jealousy

LuCxeed Poem

Easy to be produced,
to reproduce
Affected cells sextupled,
decupled
Overactive,
overwhelmingly powerful
In mixing emotion and action
In messing up truth, untruth,,
or goodness
Poison others, ruin with
assuming senses
Avenge even at
no one's benefit

Chemistry of Jealousy

Tragic blood, tragic tears
Run a tragic river
Horrifying - dark and red
And scream of innocent souls
From ancient time
    to every corner
Of modernity
All due to
    Chemistry of Jealousy

LuCxeed Poem

chemistry to jealousy

Chemistry of Jealousy

Where is the stop
A doctor beyond a doctor
Continuing to concentrate
After half a century
In a lab, huge with formidable
Data without verge
What is the cure

Me and

Gentle touch on my face
Gentle touch on my hands
Immense peace
Mysterious romance

I'd rather stroll on and on
    and on
Had no duty called
Had nothing to be done

Me and Drizzle

Drizzle

Mistlike finest droplets drop
From nowhere, wrap me up
With mystique in dew drops
Zillions. None of them stops

We stroll on and on.
Me and Drizzle
Everything seems nothing
But a drizzle. Dazzling

LuCxeed Poem

Catastrophe

Hurricane Katrina rages,
blows in thirty feet high flood,
burying town by town
but home's roof.
Catastrophe must be shocked
by a stark contrast -

Catastrophe Shocked

Shocked

One man dives
    into violent turbulence,
swallowed, disappears,
    reemerges, spared.
With one boat, less tiny
    than a grain seed
in the windstorm, one man
    wrestles with the tempest
for victims from
    brink of death,
    one, two, eight, ten...

LuCxeed Poem

Catastrophe

Heroic gallantry challenges
raging hurricane.
A singular man
has pulled out ten lives
from the snatch of death
while armed gangs
plunder and loot, ruthless,
while Insensitivity indulges
in nothingness.

Catastrophe Shocked

Shocked

The stark contrast must have
shocked Catastrophe,
yet too weak to stir
soulless numbness.
Heart of survivors is broken
by pillage, and worse,
and more... Our hero,
a man of courage,
cannot stifle
his anguished cry -

LuCxeed Poem

Catastrophe

Thousands have died.
No more boats,
no bigger boats,
in time, to save more...
Tragically shameful.

Catastrophe Shocked

Shocked

Our hero of Gallantry,
of Chivalry,
dives into violent turbulence,
swallowed, disappears,
reemerges, spared.
in the windstorm,
wrestles with the tempest,
has pulled out ten lives
from brink of death,

Catastrophe must be
shocked...

Another starlit summer night.
Another sweet time
for a chat.
Mother read and jested.
Her six year-old girl giggled,
Mommy, you're here.
Where?
Girl's chubby hand
touched her chest.
What is in there?
Mother teased.
My heart has three rooms,
Girl said,
one for Conscience,
one for Wisdom,

Met the Wisest

Mother held back her laugher.
The girl continued,
And you're in the one
for Love.
Night hushed
whistling leaves to be quiet
To listen to what a little girl
precisely said.
Clock stopped to note
a moment
To note Girl said
what she thought.
Mother was stunned to hear
Her little girl may have met
the wisest in her dream.

Met the Wisest

Do you believe
Couch is a magician,
at the center of Luxury,
chubby, solidly heavy,
to spare muscle's energy,
relieve intensity,
to feed the desire for Ego,
soothe anxiety?

COUCH

Couch Magician

Couch mushrooms.
Couch is carried in,
escorted and worshiped
like an ancient Queen,
or King,
claims spacious space
without dither
to dutifully coach folks
to ease their manner.

MAGICIAN

An outstanding magician.
Unchallenged popularity
and longevity.
Stylish, lavish,
ever in fashion.
As like mine?
Believe me. Mighty,
posing and imposing.
Stately impression.

COUCH

Couch Magician

The perpetual leather elegance
is nearly a signature
*   of significance*
of my home, of my office,
bearing friendly coziness,
and extravagance.

MAGICIAN

Couch Magician
nurtures confidence,
hours each day,
days each month,
luxuriates in my comfort
when I team up with
my sports team on television,
and of course in conversation,

COUCH.

till an alerting moment.
Gazing at self
in the mirror trying on a suit
once a perfect fit.
Left and right, front and back.
How not alright?
Kidding me, who doubled
my chin again?
Unfaithful mirrors,
concealing truthfulness.

MAGICIAN

Really, I consider myself
a manly man.
To my dismay, the mirror
distorts my portrait.
I'm not obsessed by ego.
Healthy, aren't I?
The mirror seems
not to suggest so.
My mood, along with
my comfort zone, subsides.

COUCH

Couch Magician

Who else could be blamed
for the irresistible temptation,
and for an unpleasant
reputation?
Too good. Who sinks into it,
who'll spring out as
chubby Couch Potato.

A bitter and sweet
Magician.

MAGICIAN

The moonlight is never tired
Of lighting my playground,
Circles around my bed,
caresses my forehead,
Soothes me into
a star-twinkled world
Embellished with
enchantments.
Again and again
over decades.

Silver Crown

The sunlight has dyed
my hair golden brown,
Shone upon my way
all years round.
The heart constantly sings
her triumphant song -
A poetic soul is ever young,
ever young.
Though soon the snow,
the moon
Is to give me a silver crown.

Jove cannot slow down
his brilliant horse carriage.
Galaxy will not run
the Milky Way
with less charge.
Pick up the seeds
radiating in dreams.

Silver Crown

Catch the sunrise as birds
chirp in early mornings.
Catch the moonlight.
Let flight fetch the winds.
Time will be, and make
a forest beneath,
your wings.

LuCxeed Poem

*Dyllon, have you heard
the cry
Of our unborn child,
Of your unborn son?
Have you heard my cry,
your bride
At the coming wedding?
You asked me to marry you,
holding
My hand...*

"...isn't so planned..."

Dyllon -
My darling, my dearest,
My unwed husband,
Father of our child,
Father of our unborn son,
Our life isn't so planned.
No--. It is not--.
This is not what we've
promised... No...

"Planned"

LuCxeed Poem

Dyllon -
Can you hear me?
Can you hear your son
Named after you?
Can you hear
Him kicking in my belly,
Clamoring to see you?
My dear,
Baby Dyllon is weeping
with me...

"...isn't so planned..."

"My dearest unwed wife...,
My dearest unborn child..."
Muffled by cries,
voice from inside
The flag-draped coffin
is shaken;
Death won't let
Dyllon continue...
Muffled by cries,
voice from inside
The flag-draped coffin is
cut off. Broken.

Planned"

LuCxeed Poem

Inside, withered,
is blood of life.
Outside, like a river,
flow tears of grief,
From the cry of an unborn
child for his father,
From the cry of a pregnant
Woman for her
unwed husband.
Coffin's almost failed to
bear... but wept,
Hiding beneath
the draped flag, also wet.

"...isn't so planned..."

Between the hearts,
inside, quiet,
And outside, tormented,
The flag-draped coffin
mourns
With a barely-heard sound -
"Dyllon hears you no more.
Though he must want to hug,
to beg
You two: Be strong. Live on.

Cry no more."

Planned"

LuCxeed Poem

Nature's Touch

Nature's Touch

Little as I once was,
Catching falling leaves,
climbing fallen trees,
I wondered
where Nature was.
It seemed far, and far,
and beyond reach.

LuCxeed Poem

As a grown-up,
I ever fail to count
Nature's hues,
just too much,
And much richer
than rich.
Yellow is greenish,
Blue is purplish,
and such. And such.

Nature's Touch

Now, all by sudden,
I sense peonies' light,
light's life,
redwoods' speech.
Butterfly pats my hat.
Perching magpies
and I side by side.
I am wordless, touched
by Nature's touch.

Touch

LuCxeed Poem

Don't Go Away

Don't Go Away

I'll see you no more,
though I've never
    seen you before.
You left Life... "How so?"
Pain lingers on shore.
    Eyes sore.

The water is icy cold.
Hopelessness holds
your eyes open,
    unable to rest, to close.
Sorrowful, lifeless
    blue crystals, stoic.

"Don't Go Away"

Don't Go Away

Your car honks,
calling you ashore;
fish try to push you back
where you belong.
You hear them no more.
Is Hope dead
before Soul is gone?

River grieves,
cleansing you with eddies.
Wind wails,
burying you with leaves.
I pray
"please do not go away"
(it comes too late), in vain.

LuCxeed Poem

Unless ...

Love is voice of song
wings of bird
aura of fragrance
carriage of romance

Love holds the key
to Paradise
where Spring conjures
infinite new life
Summer splashes around
without a raincoat
Autumn chuckles
amidst golden leaves

Unless...

Sacredly true,
as Love always is
(unless it is not Love)
everywhere Love goes
(unless one lets Love leave)

Not once, not twice
I was there, twirling in music
not in a dream,
tasting Paradise
of Love in gentle breeze

How much Liberty
do I have
to choose my parents
to choose my siblings
to choose my childhood
to choose my primary school
to choose my teachers
to choose heaven or hell
to choose today or tomorrow

Seemingly
(if not for all of us)
Fate rolls the dice

Fate Rolls The Dice i

LuCxeed Poem

Fate showers a child
with love but no free will
Fate bestows the child
a fortune
when Wealth is a curse
Knowledge pollutes
Into somewhere
without choice
out of nowhere the boy grows
to learn to make his own move

Is it possible
when Fate rolls the dice
(if not for all of us)
we deliver our own move

Fate Rolls The Dice .ii.

www.ingramcontent.com/pod-product-compliance
Lightning Source LLC
Chambersburg PA
CBHW030111240426
43673CB00002B/37
* 9 7 8 1 9 3 3 1 8 7 5 7 0 *